For my daughter, Hannah

First published in the United States of America in 2006 by Walker Publishing Company, Inc.
Distributed to the trade by Holtzbrinck Publishers

For information about permission to reproduce selections from this book, write to
Permissions, Walker & Company, 104 Fifth Avenue, New York, New York 10011

Library of Congress Cataloging-in-Publication Data available upon request
LCCN: 2006044702

ISBN-10: 0-8027-9563-3 • ISBN-13: 978-0-8027-9563-2 (hardcover)
ISBN-10: 0-8027-9564-1 • ISBN-13: 978-0-8027-9564-9 (reinforced)

The illustrations for this book were created using pencil, pen, brush, India ink, bristol board and computer.

Book design by John Candell

Visit Walker & Company's Web site at www.walkeryoungreaders.com

Printed in the U.S.A. by Worzalla

4 6 8 10 9 7 5 3 (hardcover)
2 4 6 8 10 9 7 5 3 (reinforced)

All papers used by Walker & Company are natural, recyclable products
made from wood grown in well-managed forests. The manufacturing processes
conform to the environmental regulations of the country of origin.

GONE WILD

AN ENDANGERED ANIMAL ALPHABET

DAVID McLIMANS

WALKER & COMPANY ❋ NEW YORK

INTRODUCTION

Our planet is home to so many plants and animals that it is impossible to know exactly how many species are sharing the earth with us. So far, scientists have named and described almost 1.5 million species, yet ninety percent of plants and invertebrates still haven't been identified. Over time, people have taken over more and more wild places, creating challenges and dangers for the other creatures sharing those spaces. There are more than 5,000 animals facing extinction today.

The twenty-six endangered animals featured were selected because they presented visual opportunities. Our alphabet's letters developed over centuries from pictures and symbols. Picture writing, or pictograms, represented the object being portrayed. In a way, this alphabet is a return to picture writing. The challenge for me in creating these images was finding endangered animals whose shape and form fit naturally together with the letters that begin their names. Except for the letter X, all letters correspond to the animals' common name. For X, the scientific, or Latin, name is used.

The earth is an amazing, beautiful, wondrous, diverse, and fragile planet. By protecting and saving animals and their habitats, we are also protecting ourselves.

Here is a more detailed explanation of the categories appearing in each animal's vital statistics for a better understanding of the threat level facing each species profiled in *Gone Wild*:

CRITICALLY ENDANGERED

Extremely high risk of extinction in the wild in the immediate future:
A reduction of at least eighty percent, projected or suspected to be met in the next ten years or three generations.

ENDANGERED

Very high risk of extinction in the wild in the near future:
A reduction of at least fifty percent, projected to be met in the next ten years or three generations.

VULNERABLE

High risk of extinction in the wild during the medium-term future:
A reduction of at least twenty percent, projected to be met within the next ten years or three generations.

A a

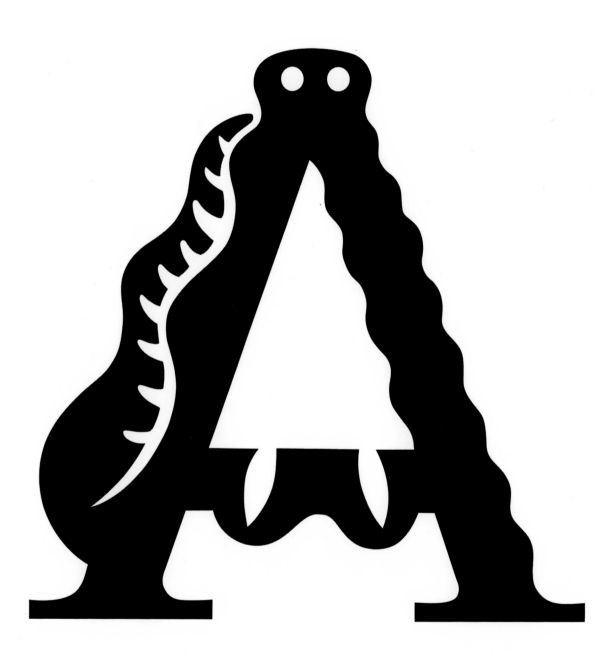

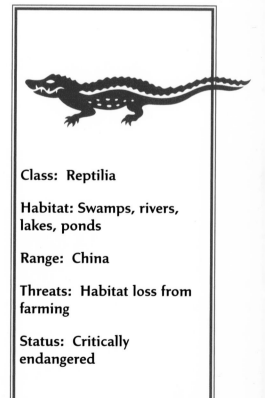

Class: Reptilia

Habitat: Swamps, rivers, lakes, ponds

Range: China

Threats: Habitat loss from farming

Status: Critically endangered

B b

Class: Reptilia

Habitat: Tropical forest

Range: Madagascar

Threats: Habitat loss from farming

Status: Vulnerable

C c

Class: Actinopterygii

Habitat: Subtropical freshwater

Range: Northern Patagonia

Threats: Habitat loss

Status: Endangered

D d

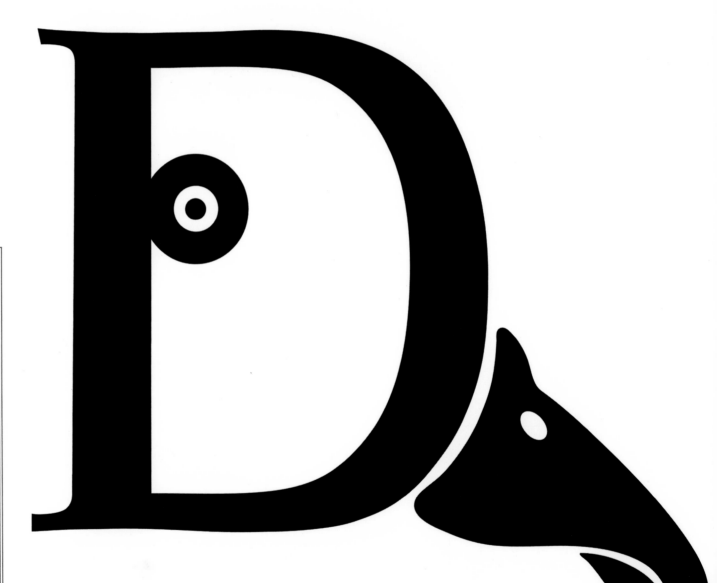

Class: Aves

Habitat: Wetlands, temperate forests, rivers, streams

Range: New Zealand

Threats: Habitat loss, introduction of new predator

Status: Endangered

E e

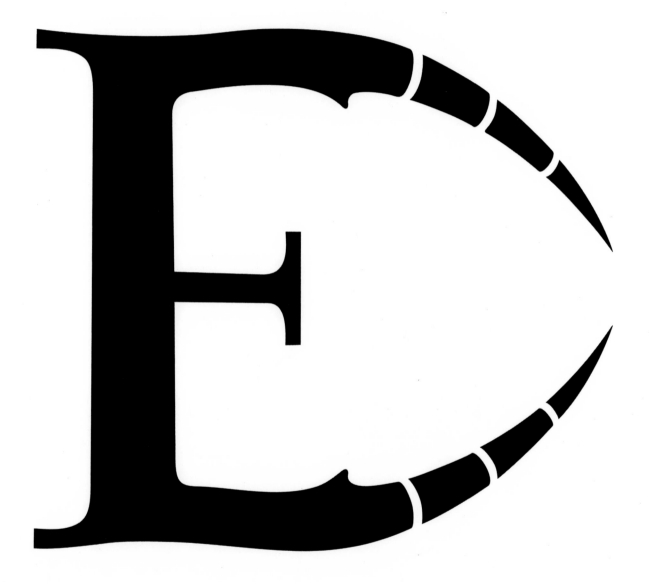

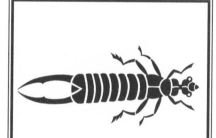

Class: Insecta

Habitat: Tropical scrub and woodlands

Range: St. Helena Island

Threats: Habitat loss, localized climate change

Status: Critically endangered

F f

Class: Aves

Habitat: High plateau, cold desert, lakes

Range: Argentina, Chile, Bolivia, Peru

Threats: Mining, egg harvesting, tourism

Status: Vulnerable

G g

Class: Aves

Habitat: Deltas, lakes, marshes, streams

Range: China, Japan, Korea, Mongolia, Russia

Threats: Habitat loss, hunting, water pollution

Status: Critically endangered

BUSHMAN HARE *Bunolagus monticularis*

H h

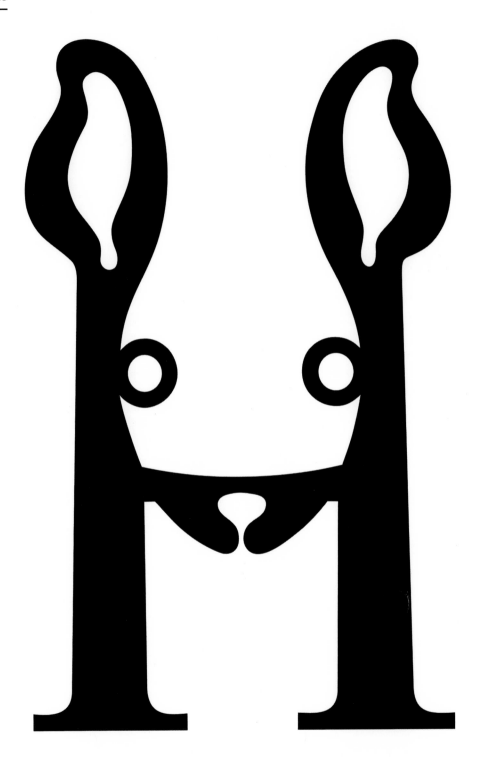

Class: Mammalia

Habitat: Scrubland

Range: South Africa

Threats: Habitat loss from farming, hunting, wild cats and dogs

Status: Critically endangered

I i

Class: Aves

Habitat: Wetlands, lakes, streams, temperate forest

Range: China, Japan, Korea

Threats: Pollution, habitat loss

Status: Endangered

FLORIDA SCRUB-JAY *Aphelocoma coerulescens*

J j

Class: Aves

Habitat: Scrubland, chaparral

Range: Florida, Mexico

Threats: Habitat loss from farming and human development

Status: Vulnerable

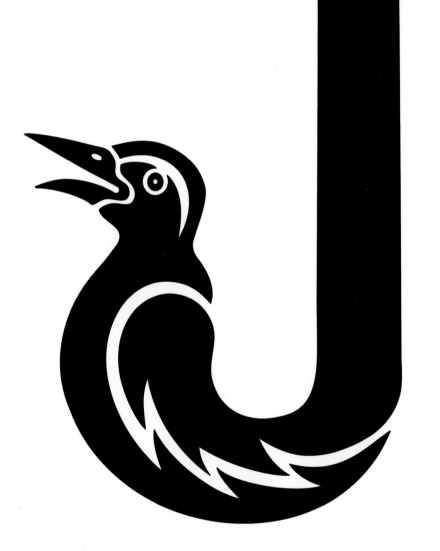

K k

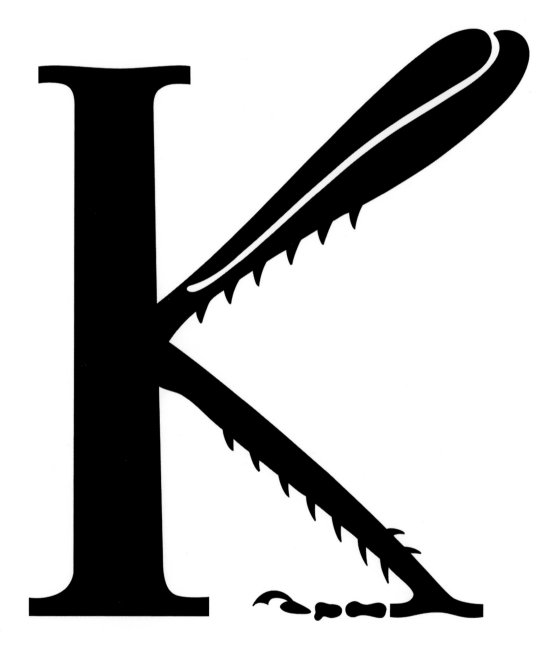

Class: Insecta

Habitat: Tropical rain forest, temperate forest, grassland

Range: Florida

Threats: Habitat loss

Status: Vulnerable

L l

Class: Mammalia

Habitat: Alpine

Range: Russia, Mongolia, China, Tibet, Afghanistan, Pakistan, India

Threats: Poaching, habitat loss, prey loss, hunting

Status: Endangered

M m

Class: Insecta

Habitat: Prairie

Range: Southwestern United States

Threats: Habitat loss, chemical pollution

Status: Critically endangered

N n

Class: Amphibia

Habitat: Freshwater wetlands, lakes

Range: Southern United States, Mexico

Threats: Habitat loss from farming, water pollution

Status: Endangered

O o

Class: Aves

Habitat: Old-growth forest, temperate forest

Range: Canada, Mexico, Western United States

Threats: Habitat loss, logging, encroachment of barred owls

Status: Vulnerable

PIPING PLOVER   *Charadrius melodus*

P p

Class: Aves

Habitat: Wetland

Range: Caribbean Islands, Cuba, Mexico, Great Lakes, Atlantic coast, Gulf coast regions of the United States

Threats: Habitat loss from development

Status: Vulnerable

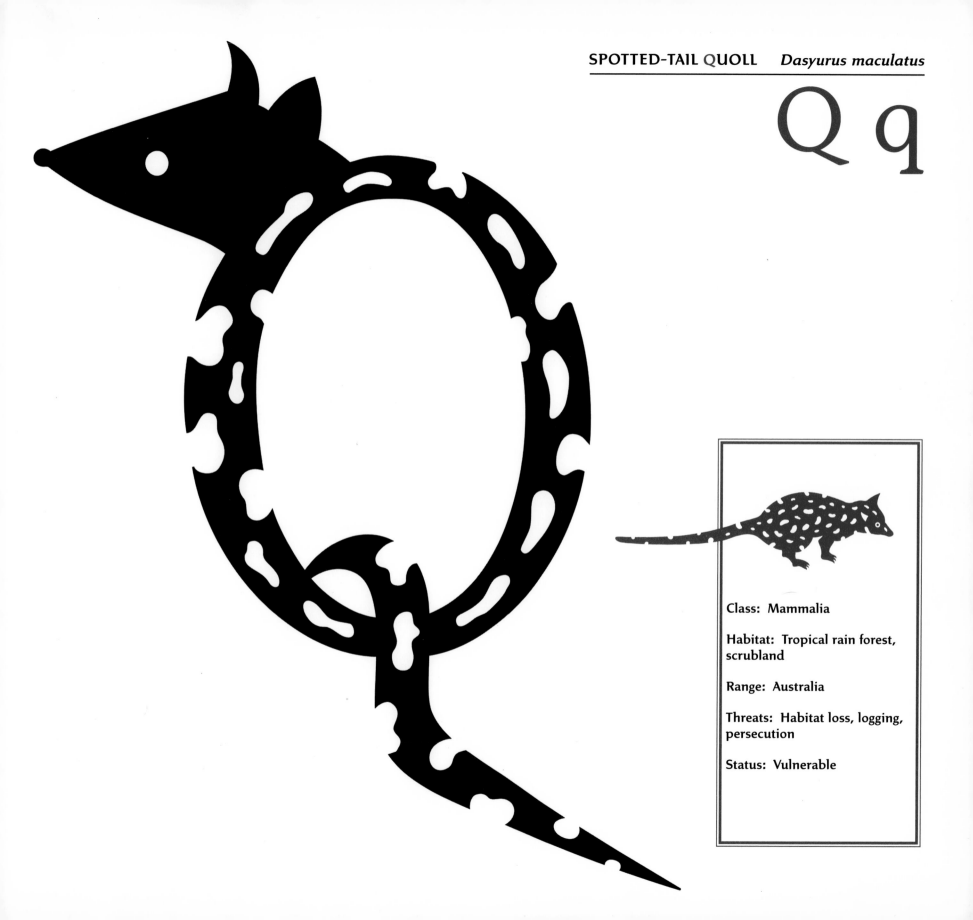

SPOTTED-TAIL QUOLL   *Dasyurus maculatus*

Q q

Class: Mammalia

Habitat: Tropical rain forest, scrubland

Range: Australia

Threats: Habitat loss, logging, persecution

Status: Vulnerable

BLACK RHINOCEROS   *Diceros bicornis*

R r

Class: Mammalia

Habitat: Savanna, scrubland, desert

Range: Cameroon, Chad, Namibia, South Africa, Kenya, Zimbabwe

Threats: Poaching for horn trade, civil war, habitat changes

Status: Critically endangered

ORIENTAL WHITE **STORK**   *Ciconia boyciana*

S s

Class: Aves

Habitat: Temperate forests, wetlands, coastline, tidal flats

Range: Bangladesh, China, India, Japan, Korea, Mongolia, Myanmar, Philippines, Russia, Taiwan

Threats: Habitat loss, deforestation, wetland drainage, farming

Status: Endangered

T t

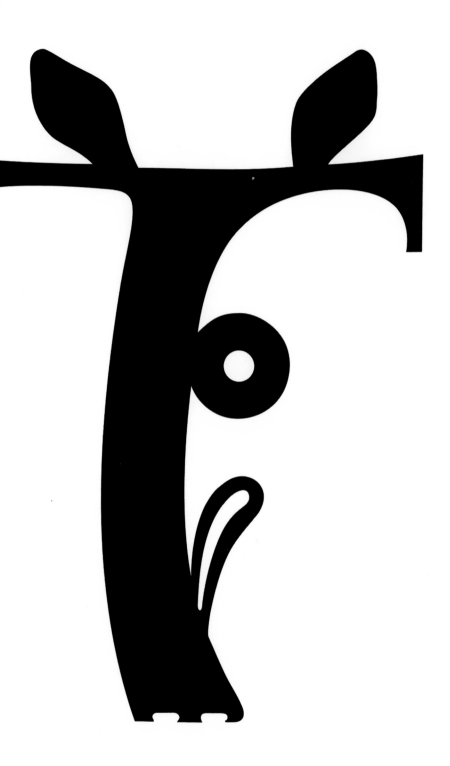

Class: Mammalia

Habitat: Alpine, chaparral, cloud forest, riverine meadow

Range: Columbia, Ecuador, Peru

Threats: Habitat loss from farming, mining, logging, hunting

Status: Endangered

U u

Class: Mammalia

Habitat: Tropical rain forest

Range: Brazil, Columbia

Threats: Habitat loss, logging, hunting, pet trade

Status: Vulnerable

V v

Class: Mammalia

Habitat: Grasslands

Range: Iran

Threats: Habitat loss from farming

Status: Endangered

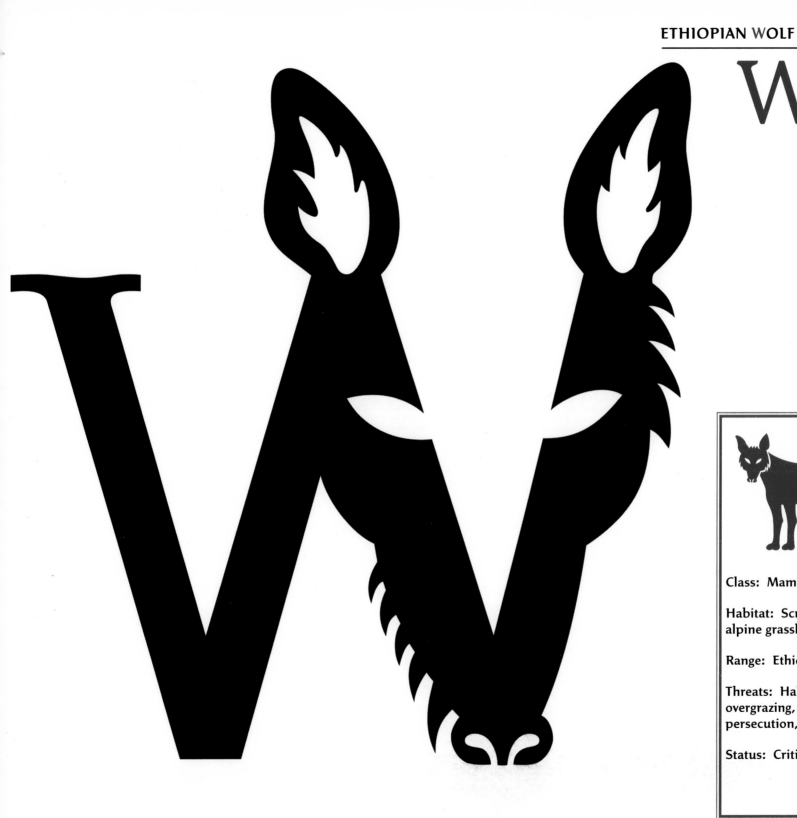

ETHIOPIAN WOLF *Canis simensis*

W w

Class: Mammalia

Habitat: Scrubland, grassland, alpine grassland

Range: Ethiopia

Threats: Habitat loss, overgrazing, human persecution, warfare

Status: Critically endangered

Xenopus gilli   (CAPE CLAWED FROG)

X x

Class: Amphibia

Habitat: Wetlands, marshes

Range: South Africa

Threats: Habitat loss,
urbanization, hybridization

Status: Endangered

Y y

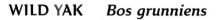

Class: Mammalia

Habitat: Alpine tundra, cold desert

Range: Tibet, China, India, Nepal

Threats: Habitat loss, hunting, inbreeding with domestic yaks

Status: Vulnerable

Z z

Class: Mammalia

Habitat: Grasslands, savannah, plains

Range: Kenya, Somalia, Ethiopia

Threats: Hunting, poaching, overgrazing

Status: Endangered

CHINESE ALLIGATOR

Despite its fierce appearance, this alligator is actually very timid and spends much of its time hiding in burrows called "gator holes." The most serious threat to this species is people building dams and turning marshlands into farms. Farmers see the alligator as a nuisance to be eliminated and often sell its organs to make traditional Chinese medicine.

MADAGASCAR TREE BOA

The boa is a night hunter and has heat sensitive pits around its mouth enabling it to hunt for warm-blooded prey in complete darkness. It is a constrictor, with powerful coils that tighten and suffocate prey. Then by unhinging its jaw, the boa can swallow the catch whole. Because of human settlement only fifteen percent of its original habitat remains.

NAKED CHARACIN

Naked, for this unusual fish, means that it has no scales. Perhaps even more amazing is that it is found in only one place in the world: Northern Patagonia in Argentina. The fish survive in this cold, isolated environment by living in warm, thermally heated mountain creeks. But their population is decreasing due to the limited number of warm water creeks.

BLUE DUCK

Thanks to its large webbed feet, the blue duck can move easily through swift rapids and climb over large boulders. It also dives into powerful currents, where its feet cling to boulders while feeding underwater. The blue duck is one of the most endangered waterfowl, with only 2,000-4,000 birds left in the wild. Trout competing for the same food source are currently their greatest threat to survival.

ST. HELENA EARWIG

The myth that earwigs crawl into a sleeping person's ear is probably how this bug got its name. These rare giant earwigs can only be found on St. Helena, a remote island where Napoleon spent the last years of his life in exile. Deforestation has almost completely destroyed the island's lush tropical wilderness. No one has seen one of these rare insects in the wild since 1965.

ANDEAN FLAMINGO

The Andean flamingo is marked by vibrant yellow legs and extraordinary bills that have rows of horny strainers to suck in water and food. Gathering around the world's highest volcanoes, they crowd near hot springs and salty lakes to survive the cold. Drought conditions, borax mining, and egg harvesting threaten their population.

SWAN GOOSE

This goose is named for its long swanlike back and neck. Geese are sometimes called "honkers," and the swan goose's honk, or call, is loud and hardy. They are friendlier than other geese, but this has endangered them because staying close to people leads to unrestricted hunting and egg collection. Wetland destruction has also contributed to their rapid decline.

BUSHMAN HARE

This hare is one of the rarest mammals on the planet, found only in dense brush along rivers in South Africa's central Karoo Region. With approximately 250 left in the wild, it is almost extinct. Being a fast runner and a strong jumper has not been enough to protect these hares. Habitat loss and direct threats from hunting, trapping, and wild cats and dogs endanger their population.

CRESTED IBIS

One of the fifty rarest birds in the world, this bird's extraordinary beauty has led to the threat of extinction. It was systematically hunted for its long white plumes, which were used to decorate women's hats. Despite strict laws and captive breeding programs, the crested ibis is extinct in most of its habitat. It is now only found in the Shaanxi Provence of China, where fewer than fifty birds remain.

FLORIDA SCRUB-JAY

The Florida scrub where this jay lives is one of the most endangered environments in North America because of rapid development. Because they mate for life and are fiercely territorial, attempts to relocate Florida scrub-jays have not been very successful. As their habitat disappears, their numbers dwindle. There are only about 2,000 jays left in the wild.

KEYS SHORT-WINGED CONEHEAD KATYDID

Katydids are in the grasshopper family, which contains over 6,800 species. Like grasshoppers, they are excellent jumpers and are well camouflaged. With oversized jaws, they are able to eat the tough leaves in saw and cabbage palmettos. Keys short-winged coneheads cannot fly and have no way of traveling long distances. This probably contributes to their threatened status.

SNOW LEOPARD

These powerful hunters can jump on prey over forty feet away and bring down animals two or three times its size. Snow leopards are not closely related to other leopards, except in name, and therefore cannot roar or purr. Because they live atop high mountain peaks, their exact numbers are not known. Poaching for their fur and the decline of larger prey are serious threats to their survival.

PRAIRIE SPHINX MOTH

One of the most incredible things about moths is the way they change from crawling, leaf-munching caterpillars into delicate, winged adults. Adult moths feed on flower nectar, and in May and June, they can be seen in groups (or broods) flying over sand washes and prairie blowouts. Insecticide spraying is an ongoing threat to this rare, beautiful moth.

BLACK-SPOTTED NEWT

Little is known about this species. Like tadpoles, their young have gills and always live underwater. Adults can be found in and around pools, ponds, and swamps. Newts must always stay moist or they die. When water is scarce, they crawl under damp logs to survive. Once common in Texas, they are now endangered due to water pollution, insecticide, and herbicide use.

SPOTTED OWL

With sharp eyesight and wing feathers that allow them to fly silently, these owls are ideal nighttime hunters. Most spotted owls live in old growth forests, which have been allowed to grow freely for more than 200 years. There have been many conflicts between environmentalists trying to save this owl and loggers dependant on being able to cut old growth trees for their livelihoods.

PIPING PLOVER

The piping plover is a tiny, hard-to-spot shorebird. In the late 1800s and early 1900s, large numbers were shot for sport and hat decorations, which pushed them to the edge of extinction. In 1918, The Migratory Bird Treaty made it illegal to hunt them. Though saved from extinction, their population has never recovered.

SPOTTED-TAIL QUOLL

With a strong body and teeth, this fierce marsupial attacks medium-sized mammals by biting the back of the skull or neck. It is a night hunter and communicates using a variety of hisses, cries, and screams. Since the 1990s, its numbers have declined dramatically. As forests are increasingly opened up for logging, this quoll might be unable to survive.

BLACK RHINOCEROS

One of the largest free-roaming mammals left on earth, rhinos are important to the ecosystem because they eat a variety of plants (which can take up to three days to digest), transport them, and then deposit them as droppings that end up getting planted. Although protected, they are often killed for their horns, which are used as a fever-reducing ingredient in traditional Chinese medicine.

ORIENTAL WHITE STORK

These solitary birds like to build nests high up in forests, giving them a good view of the surrounding area. Extinct in Japan, South and North Korea as a wild breeding bird, their total population was estimated at 2,500 in the 1990s. The Three Gorges dam project, in China's Hubei province, will endanger many parts of the stork's wintering ground when completed.

ANDEAN TAPIR

This long-snouted relative of the horse inhabits forests high in the Andes Mountains, with a preference for moist habitats where it can bathe often. Land clearing for agriculture and livestock are the main causes of the Andean tapirs' decline. Highland Indians use tapirs' hooves and snouts as medicinal remedies for epilepsy and heart problems, devastating the surviving population.

BALD-HEADED UAKARI

The bald uakari has a face that changes color, from pink to red, depending on its mood. Being a treetop specialist, it rarely touches the ground. They are hunted for meat in Peru and for bait in Brazil, where they are not eaten because their faces look too human. They are extinct in much of their former range in Peru because of hunting and logging.

BALUCHISTAN VOLE

Voles are rodents, and forty percent of all mammals in the world are rodents. Despite a bad reputation, voles are ecologically important and provide a vital food source for many predatory animals. But to the farmer, they are crop-destroying pests to be eliminated. As more and more land is cultivated for farming and housing, their numbers continue to decline.

ETHIOPIAN WOLF

Ethiopian wolves live in a very small territory, confined to isolated grasslands in the mountains of Ethiopia. There are fewer than 500 Ethiopian wolves left due to overgrazing and competition with wild dogs. As their population gets smaller, wolves have begun to mate with wild dogs, which is also a threat to their survival as a species.

XENOPUS GILLI (CAPE CLAWED FROG)

The *xenopus gilli* is an unusual frog: it has no tongue, and only lives in cold, black, acid water. Found only in the southwestern region of South Africa, where it has become one of the most endangered amphibians in the world, the *xenopus gilli* is very sensitive to changes in water chemistry. Land development and dam construction have destroyed many of this frog's natural habitats.

WILD YAK

Wild yaks have adapted to live at high altitudes and harsh conditions with many more blood cells helping their bodies carry more oxygen. They also have thick coats and a low number of sweat glands, which helps conserve body heat. Once found throughout the entire Tibetan plateau, its range has now been cut in half due to competition with ranchers raising domestic livestock.

GREVY'S ZEBRA

The Grevy's Zebra spends up to eighty percent of its time eating. Although it can survive both extreme heat and thirst, and has very keen eyesight and hearing, its population has declined by seventy percent in Kenya. They have always been hunted for their beautiful striped hide, but competition with domestic livestock and overgrazing are the main reasons their numbers continue to decline.

To learn more about organizations that help endangered animals, check out these Web sites:

WORLD WILDLIFE FUND • *www.worldwildlife.org*

WILDAID • *www.wildaid.org*

DEFENDERS OF WILDLIFE • *www.kidsplanet.org*

AMERICAN MUSEUM OF NATURAL HISTORY • *www.amnh.org/nationalcenter/Endangered/*

THE SIERRA CLUB • *www.sierraclub.org*

WORLD CONSERVATION UNION • *www.iucn.org*

ENDANGERED SPECIES COALITION • *www.stopextinction.org*

THE NATURE CONSERVANCY • *www.nature.org*

EARTHTRUST • *www.earthtrust.org*

CONSERVATION INTERNATIONAL • *www.conservation.org*

For Further Reading

Bailey, Jill and Clint Twist. *Endangered Animals A-Z.* New York: Blackbirch Press, 2004.

Cogger, Harold G., Joseph Forshaw, Edwin Gould, George McKay, and Richard G. Zweifel, eds. *Encyclopedia of Animals: Mammals, Birds, Reptiles, Amphibians.* San Francisco: Fog City Press, 1993.

Fichter, George S. and Kristin Kest. *Endangered Animals.* New York: St. Martin's Press, 2001.

Hinshaw Patent, Dorothy and William Muñoz (illustrator). *Biodiversity.* New York: Clarion, 1996.

MacKay, Richard. *The Penguin Atlas of Endangered Species: A Worldwide Guide to Plants and Animals.* New York: Penguin, 2002.

Nowak, Ronald M. *Walker's Mammals of the World.* 2 vols. 6th ed. Baltimore: The Johns Hopkins University Press, 1999.

Perols, Sylvaine, Gallimard Jeunesse, and Wendy Barish. *Endangered Animals.* New York: Scholastic, 1997.